Copyright © 2020 Clavis Publishing Inc., New York

Originally published as *Wonderwaar. Hoe de aarde beweegt*
in Belgium and the Netherlands by Clavis Uitgeverij, 2019
English translation from the Dutch by Clavis Publishing Inc., New York

Visit us on the Web at www.clavis-publishing.com.

How the Continents Move written by Jan Leyssens and illustrated by Joachim Sneyers

ISBN 978-1-60537-580-9

This book was printed in July 2020 at Nikara, M. R. Štefánika 858/25, 963 01 Krupina, Slovakia.

First Edition
10 9 8 7 6 5 4 3 2 1

Clavis Publishing supports the First Amendment and celebrates the right to read.

HOW THE
Continents
MOVE

Written by Jan Leyssens
Illustrated by Joachim Sneyers

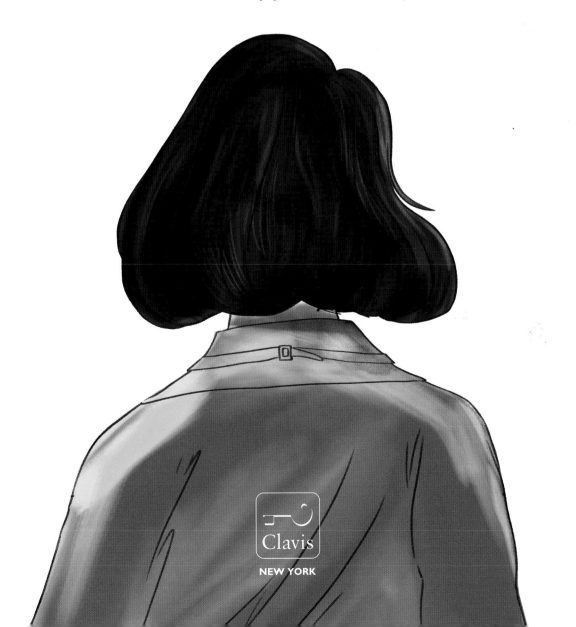

Clavis
NEW YORK

Many centuries ago, a scientist named Abraham Ortels noticed that the coastlines of the different continents could fit together, just like a puzzle. But it wasn't until the early 1900s that we began to understand why that was the case.

In 1912, another scientist, Alfred Wegener, investigated how it could be possible that the same kinds of rocks and fossils could be found on different continents, even with an entire ocean between them.

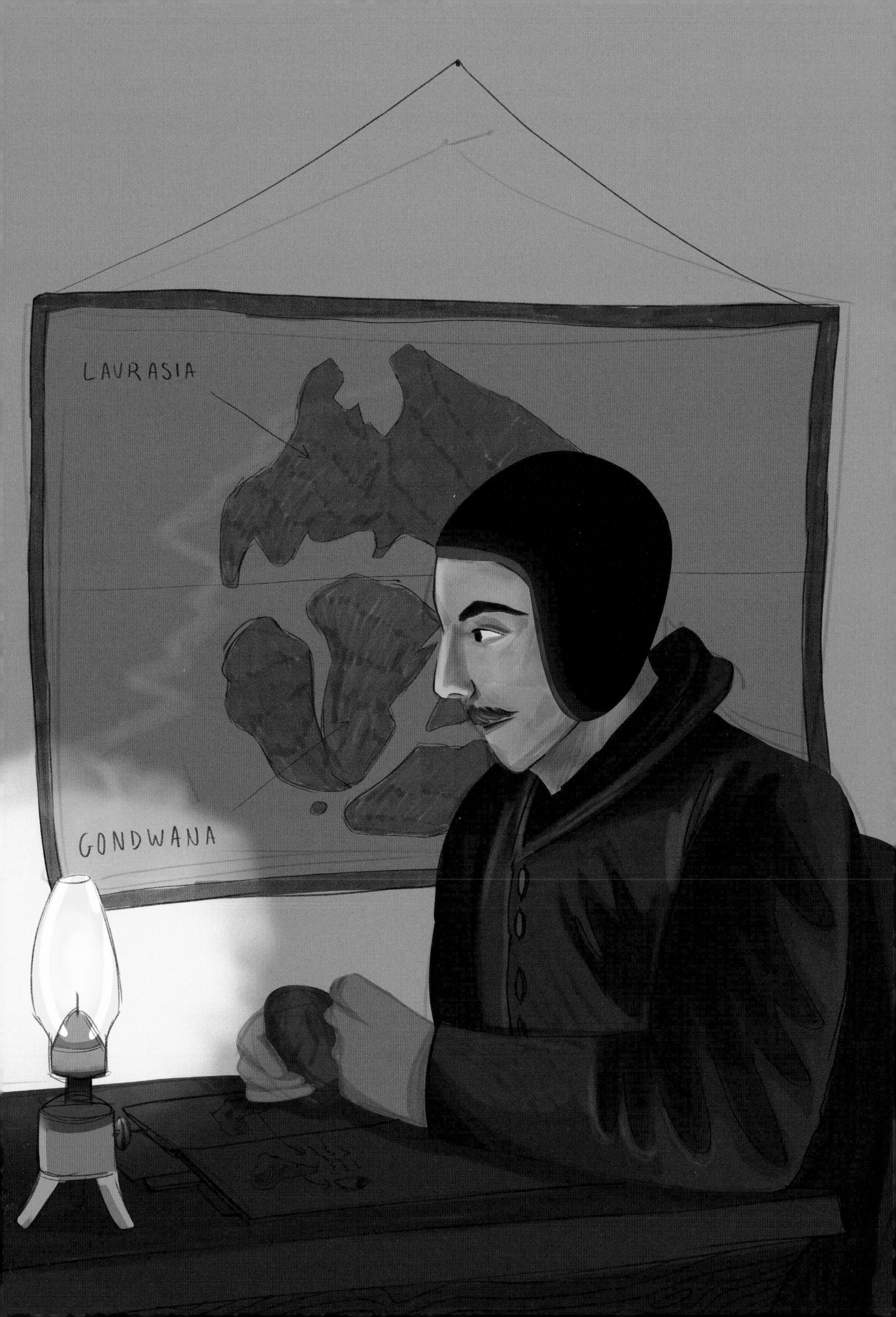
LAURASIA
GONDWANA

Alfred believed that all the continents may had been connected long ago, and then had slowly been separated into the continents we now know. He called this idea continental drift. And although Alfred found a lot of evidence showing that his theory might have been true, he couldn't tell how or why this drift took place. Moreover, the whole idea was so new that almost no scientist believed in Alfred's theory.

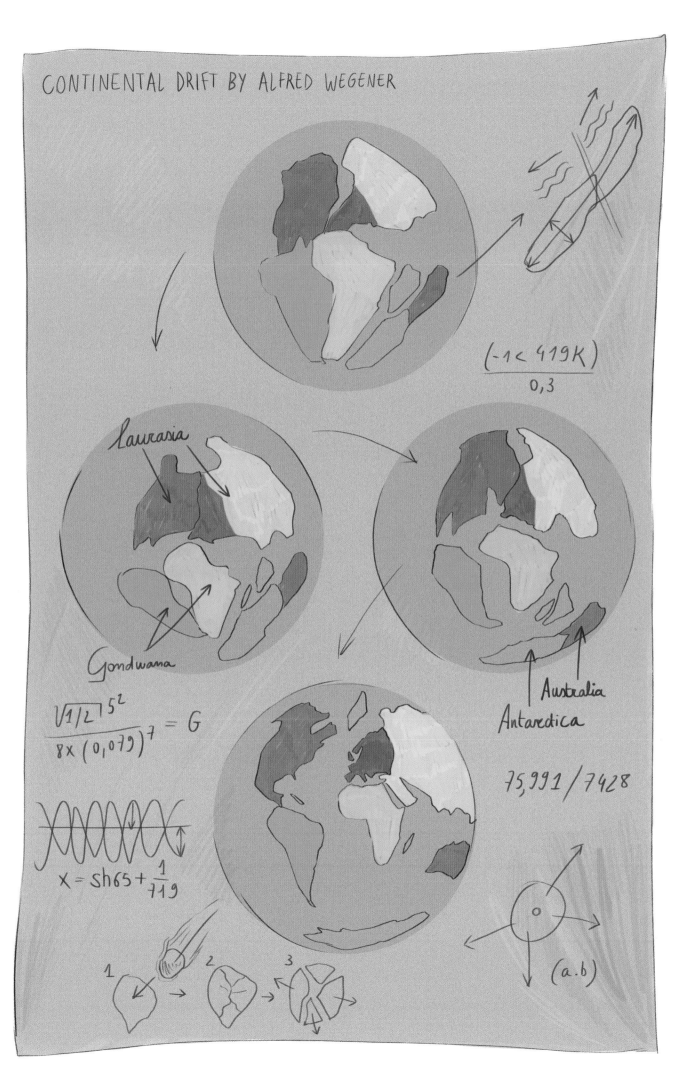

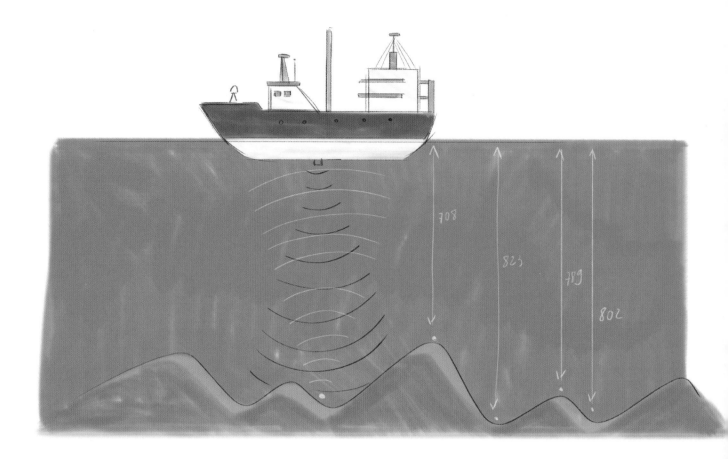

In 1943, Marie Tharp was working at Colombia University as
Bruce Heezen's assistant. Bruce had sailed around the world and
explored the bottom of the ocean using sonar to search for wrecks of
submarines and planes that had crashed. Using Bruce's measurements,
Marie drew the first map of the ocean floor. And while drawing,
Marie suddenly discovered a pattern. Near the middle of the Atlantic
Ocean, she discovered something that looked like a tear in the bottom.

Marie drew the entire mountain chain at the bottom of the ocean and called it the Mid-Atlantic Ridge. She had heard of Alfred Wegener and his theory of continental drift and discussed with Bruce whether the mountain chain might be proof that the continents had indeed been torn apart. But Bruce, like almost all of his colleagues, didn't believe in continental drift.

Marie didn't give up. She studied a map that had been created by another colleague, Howard Foster. His map indicated the key areas where earthquakes and seaquakes occurred, and Marie immediately saw that the seaquakes occurred in exactly the same place as her Mid-Atlantic Ridge. It became clear to her that the ocean floor was being pushed apart by earthquakes and volcanoes . . . and so were the continents above!

With her new evidence, she went back to Bruce, who finally believed her theory. In 1957 Marie and Bruce presented her map with the Mid-Atlantic Ridge to their colleagues, along with her ideas about how earthquakes drove apart continents. But even so, few in the community believed that the continents could move.

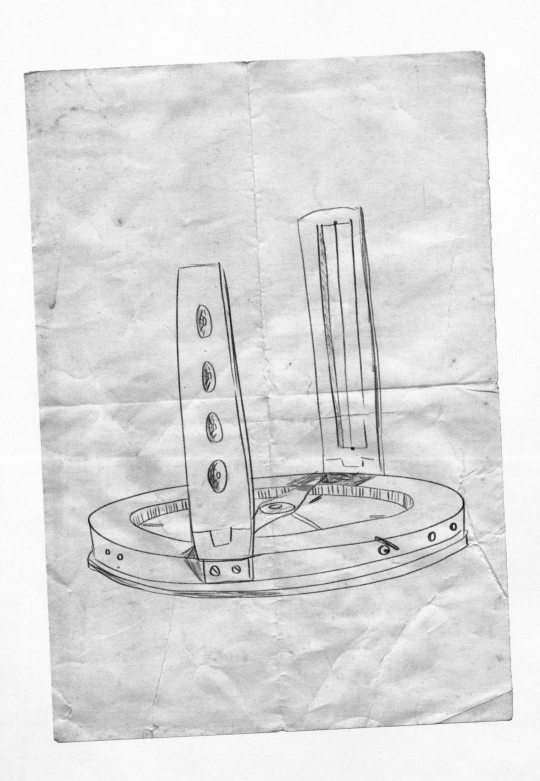

One of the most famous explorers of the time, Jacques Cousteau, proposed that he would take a boat with an underwater camera down to the bottom of the ocean. He expected to prove that the tears did not exist.

But Cousteau's recordings actually had the opposite effect. They showed that Marie was right, that there was indeed a tear in the bottom of the ocean, and that continental drift was real.

arie Tharp proved the idea of continental drift, a huge accomplishment for the science community. But it would be years before Tharp and Heezen's findings were fully accepted in the geological scientific community.

Today Marie Tharp is known as an extremely important geologist and one of the best cartographers of the last century.

CONTINENTS   FAULT LINES

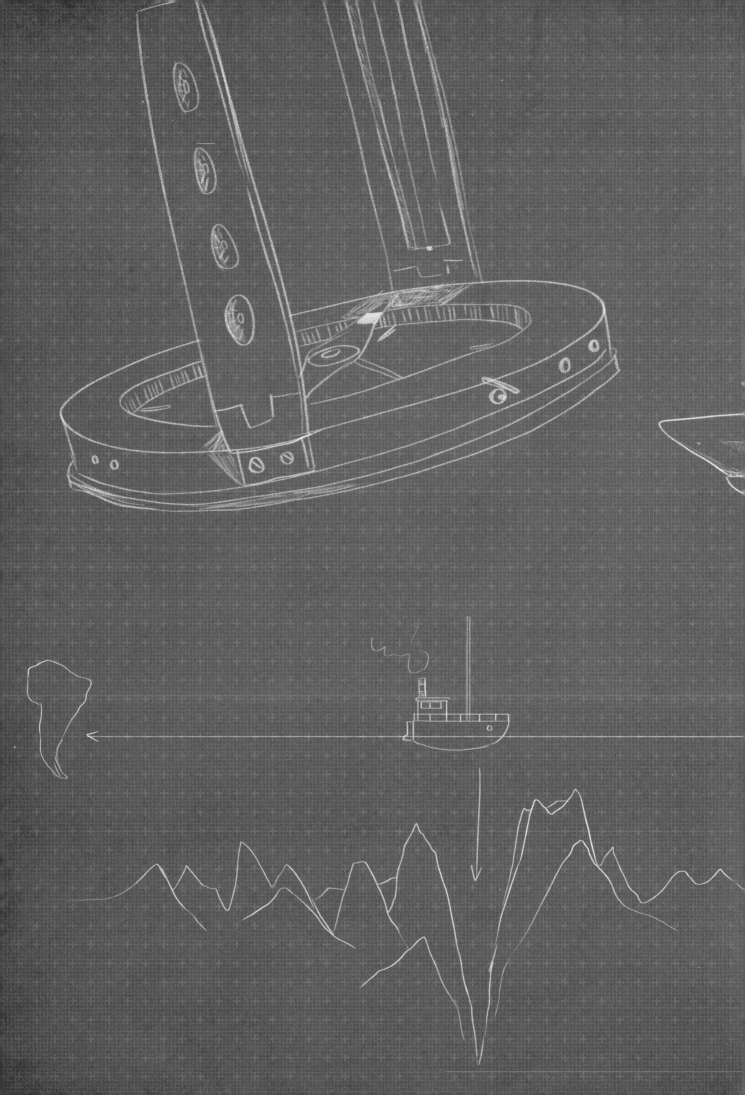